Lite Worship Services For Advent And Christmas

*Three Programs
For The Season*

Cynthia E. Cowen

CSS Publishing Company, Inc., Lima, Ohio

LITE WORSHIP SERVICES FOR ADVENT AND CHRISTMAS

Scripture quotations marked NRSV are from the *New Revised Standard Version of the Bible*, copyright 1989 by the Division of Christian Education of the National Council of the Churches of Christ in the USA. Used by permission.

Scripture quotations marked CEV are from the Contemporary English Version of the Holy Bible. Copyright © The American Bible Society 1995. Used by permission.

Scripture quotations marked NCV are from *The Youth Bible, New Century Version*, copyright © 1991 by Word Publishing, Dallas, Texas 75039. Used by permission.

For more information about CSS Publishing Company resources, visit our website at www.csspub.com.

ISBN 0-7880-1760-8   PRINTED IN U.S.A.

This book is dedicated to the many youth at Our Saviour's Lutheran Church who bring my writings to life: to my musicians, Kim and Ernie Luri, who are young, gifted, and committed Christians; to my confirmation students, who are catching a vision of what God wants from them; to my senior high youth, who are open to working with the younger students and excited about their faith; and to my college youth, who are still active in church and help out with skits whenever they can. I would especially like to say thanks to Angela Freeman, whom I have watched grow in her faith since coming to this church. She is my "Angela the Christmas Angel" in the Christmas Eve worship, We Welcome The Light Of Christmas. *Upon all of these young Christians I ask the Lord's blessing.*

Table Of Contents

Prepare Your Heart For Christmas

Foreword

Advent is a special time to prepare one's heart for Christmas. Congregations are invited through this worship resource to prepare themselves for the birth of Jesus and open their hearts to the Savior. "Prepare Your Heart For Christmas" is a service of carols and reflections which will move those who hear it to respond to the Good News of a Savior coming into our lives again.

The musical parts of the service can be highlighted by the use of a bell choir to accompany the singing or piano/organ or instrumental groups. The solo portions set the tone for a meditative mood to experience the Lord's heart of love.

Following the worship, the participants are invited to a dessert fellowship to continue being touched by the love of God with each other.

Prepare Your Heart For Christmas

Welcome And Announcements

Prelude

The Gathering Of Hearts United In Love

Call To Worship
Leader: We have come during this Advent season to prepare our hearts to receive our Lord anew. During this time in the church, we celebrate the gift the Father gave us in taking on flesh to dwell among us. Come, let us worship with hearts gathered in love.
Congregation: We come to worship the King.

Solo: "Of The Father's Love Begotten" (v. 1)

A Litany Of Love
Leader: Lord Jesus, you stood with your Father at the time of creation. Through you all things were created in love.
Congregation: Praise to Jesus, God's beloved Son.
Leader: Lord Jesus, you are the beginning and the end. Through you we find strength in this life and hope in a life to come.
Congregation: Praise to Jesus, evermore and evermore.
Leader: Lord Jesus, you are the promised Messiah. Through you we have obtained our salvation.
Congregation: Praise God for the gift of Jesus.

Solo: "Of The Father's Love Begotten" (v. 2)

A Litany Of Love
Leader: Lord God, you came to a virgin, full of grace.

Congregation: Gracious Lord, come to us, lowly sinners.
Leader: Holy Spirit, you birthed life into Mary's womb.
Congregation: Loving Spirit, birth life anew into our barren souls.
Leader: Son of God, as you looked upon your Mother Mary, look upon us this night with love.
Congregation: Jesus, we look to the manger and see the world's Savior, the face of a God who loves us.

Congregational Song: "Of The Father's Love Begotten" (v. 3)
    This is he whom seers in old time
    Chanted of with one accord,
    Whom the voices of the prophets
    Promised in their faithful word;
    Now he shines, the long expected;
    Let creation praise its Lord
    Evermore and evermore.
    — Prudentius (348-413)

A Litany Of Love
Leader: Holy Child of Bethlehem, the prophets foretold your birth.
Congregation: Let us boldly tell the world of the birth of its Savior.
Leader: Almighty God, your prophets were faithful in declaring your Word.
Congregation: Keep us strong in faith and rooted and grounded in your Holy Word.
Leader: Holy Spirit, stir our hearts to respond to God's gift of salvation.
Congregation: Come now and fill our hearts with love.

A Prayer From The Heart
Leader: Lord God, our hearts are not always right with you. Cleanse them by the power of your Holy Spirit. Purify our minds and actions. Forgive us for not desiring you as much as we want the things of this world. Only you can rescue us from sin and death. Jesus, you are Emmanuel, God with us in flesh. Send your Holy Spirit

9

into our hearts once more this Advent season that we would find your promised peace. Come, Emmanuel. Come to your people once more.

Congregation: Come, oh, come, Emmanuel. Amen.

Hearts Prepared For God's Coming

Congregational Song: "Oh, Come, Oh, Come, Emmanuel" (vv. 1, 2, 4)

Oh, come, oh, come, Emmanuel,
And ransom captive Israel,
That mourns in lonely exile here
Until the Son of God appear.
Rejoice! Rejoice! Emmanuel
Shall come to you, O Israel.

Oh, come, thou wisdom from on high,
And order all things, far and nigh;
To us the path of knowledge show,
And cause us in her ways to go.
Rejoice! Rejoice! Emmanuel
Shall come to you, O Israel.

Oh, come, thou Dayspring, come and cheer
Our spirits by Thine advent here;
Disperse the gloomy clouds of night,
And death's dark shadows put to flight.
Rejoice! Rejoice! Emmanuel
Shall come to you, O Israel.
— Latin Hymn (twelfth century)

Advent Reflection

Reading: Luke 1:67-69, 76-79 (NRSV)

Lighting Of The Advent Wreath And Reflection

10

Hearts Sing For Joy At The Birth Of Jesus

Congregational Song: "O Little Town Of Bethlehem" (vv. 1, 2)
O little town of Bethlehem,
How still we see thee lie!
Above thy deep and dreamless sleep
The silent stars go by;
Yet in thy dark streets shineth
The everlasting light;
The hopes and fears of all the years
Are met in thee tonight.

O holy Child of Bethlehem,
Descend to us we pray;
Cast out our sin, and enter in;
Be born in us today.
We hear the Christmas angels
The great glad tidings tell;
O come to us, abide with us,
Our Lord Emmanuel.
— Phillips Brooks (1835-1893)

Reflection

Reading: Micah 5:2, 4 (NRSV)

Leader

Congregational Song: "Away In A Manger" (vv. 1, 2, 3)
Away in a manger, no crib for a bed,
The little Lord Jesus laid down his sweet head;
The stars in the sky looked down where he lay,
The little Lord Jesus, asleep on the hay.

The cattle are lowing, the Baby awakes,
But little Lord Jesus no crying he makes.
I love thee, Lord Jesus, look down from the sky,
And stay by my cradle till morning is nigh.

Be near me, Lord Jesus, I ask thee to stay
Close by me forever, and love me, I pray.
Bless all the dear children in thy tender care,
And fit us for heaven to live with thee there.
— Stanzas 1 and 2, Unknown
— Stanza 3, John Thomas McFarland (1851-1913)

Reflection

Reading: Galatians 4:4-6 (NRSV)

Leader

Hearts Respond In Worship Of The Newborn King

Congregational Song: "Oh, Come, All Ye Faithful" (vv. 1, 2)
Oh, come, all ye faithful, joyful and triumphant,
Oh, come ye, oh, come ye to Bethlehem;
Come and behold him, born the king of angels;
Oh, come, let us adore him,
Oh, come, let us adore him,
Oh, come, let us adore him,
Christ the Lord!

Sing, choirs of angels, sing in exultation,
Oh, sing, all ye citizens of heaven above!
Glory to God, all glory in the highest;
Oh, come, let us adore him,
Oh, come, let us adore him,
Oh, come, let us adore him,
Christ the Lord!
— John F. Wade (1711-1786)

Reflection

Reading: John 4:23-24 (NRSV)

12

Leader

Congregational Song: "Silent Night" (vv. 1, 2, 3)
   Silent night, holy night!
   All is calm, all is bright
   Round yon virgin mother and child.
   Holy Infant, so tender and mild,
   Sleep in heavenly peace,
   Sleep in heavenly peace.

   Silent night, holy night!
   Shepherds quake at the sight;
   Glories stream from heaven afar;
   Heav'nly hosts sing, Alleluia!
   Christ, the Savior, is born!
   Christ, the Savior, is born!

   Silent night, holy night!
   Son of God, love's pure light
   Radiant beams from thy holy face,
   With the dawn of redeeming grace,
   Jesus, Lord, at thy birth,
   Jesus, Lord, at thy birth.
   — Joseph Mohr, (1792-1849)

Dismissal
Leader: Go in the love of the Son of God, born to us anew. Go in peace, and praise the Lord!
Congregation: Thanks be to God.

Postlude

Complete Resource

Prepare Your Heart For Christmas

Welcome And Announcements
(Invitation to a dessert fellowship following the worship)

Prelude

The Gathering Of Hearts United In Love

Call To Worship
Leader: We have come during this Advent season to prepare our hearts to receive our Lord anew. During this time in the church, we celebrate the gift the Father gave us in taking on flesh to dwell among us. Come, let us worship with hearts gathered in love.
Congregation: We come to worship the King.

Solo: "Of The Father's Love Begotten" (v. 1)
  Of the Father's love begotten
  Ere the worlds began to be,
  He is Alpha and Omega,
  He the source, the ending he,
  Of the things that are, that have been,
  And that future years shall see,
  Evermore and evermore.
  — Prudentius (348-413)

A Litany Of Love
Leader: Lord Jesus, you stood with your Father at the time of creation. Through you all things were created in love.
Congregation: Praise to Jesus, God's beloved Son.
Leader: Lord Jesus, you are the beginning and the end. Through you we find strength in this life and hope in a life to come.
Congregation: Praise to Jesus, evermore and evermore.

Leader: Lord Jesus, you are the promised Messiah. Through you we have obtained our salvation.
Congregation: Praise God for the gift of Jesus.

Solo: "Of The Father's Love Begotten" (v. 2)
Oh, that birth forever blessed,
When the virgin full of grace,
By the Holy Ghost conceiving,
Bore the Savior of our race,
And the babe the world's redeemer,
First revealed his sacred face,
Evermore and evermore.

A Litany Of Love
Leader: Lord God, you came to a virgin, full of grace.
Congregation: Gracious Lord, come to us, lowly sinners.
Leader: Holy Spirit, you birthed life into Mary's womb.
Congregation: Loving Spirit, birth life anew into our barren souls.
Leader: Son of God, as you looked upon your Mother Mary, look upon us this night with love.
Congregation: Jesus, we look to the manger and see the world's Savior, the face of a God who loves us.

Congregational Song: "Of The Father's Love Begotten" (v. 3)
This is he whom seers in old time
Chanted of with one accord,
Whom the voices of the prophets
Promised in their faithful word;
Now he shines, the long expected;
Let creation praise its Lord
Evermore and evermore.

A Litany Of Love
Leader: Holy Child of Bethlehem, the prophets foretold your birth.
Congregation: Let us boldly tell the world of the birth of its Savior.

Leader: Almighty God, your prophets were faithful in declaring your Word.
Congregation: Keep us strong in faith and rooted and grounded in your Holy Word.
Leader: Holy Spirit, stir our hearts to respond to God's gift of salvation.
Congregation: Come now and fill our hearts with love.

A Prayer From The Heart
Leader: Lord God, our hearts are not always right with you. Cleanse them by the power of your Holy Spirit. Purify our minds and actions. Forgive us for not desiring you as much as we want the things of this world. Only you can rescue us from sin and death. Jesus, you are Emmanuel, God with us in flesh. Send your Holy Spirit into our hearts once more this Advent season that we would find your promised peace. Come, Emmanuel. Come to your people once more.
Congregation: Come, oh, come, Emmanuel. Amen.

Hearts Prepared For God's Coming

Congregational Song: "Oh, Come, Oh, Come, Emmanuel" (vv. 1, 2, 4)
>   Oh, come, oh, come, Emmanuel,
>   And ransom captive Israel,
>   That mourns in lonely exile here
>   Until the Son of God appear.
>   *Rejoice! Rejoice! Emmanuel*
>   *Shall come to you, O Israel.*
>
>   Oh, come, thou wisdom from on high,
>   And order all things, far and nigh;
>   To us the path of knowledge show,
>   And cause us in her ways to go.
>   *Rejoice! Rejoice! Emmanuel*
>   *Shall come to you, O Israel.*

Oh, come, thou Dayspring, come and cheer
Our spirits by Thine advent here;
Disperse the gloomy clouds of night,
And death's dark shadows put to flight.
Rejoice! Rejoice! Emmanuel
Shall come to you, O Israel.
— Latin Hymn (twelfth century)

Advent Reflection

The prophet Isaiah told us that a virgin would be with child and give birth to a son, and she would call him Emmanuel, "God with us" (Isaiah 7:14). He later states that for us that child would be born; to us that son would be given. And the government of the worlds would be on his shoulders. He would have other names: Wonderful Counselor, Mighty God, Everlasting Father, Prince of Peace (Isaiah 9:6). So God's people, Israel, waited and looked for the fulfillment of that prophecy. The Advent song that we sang was Israel's prayer. It is ours as well as we await our Lord's coming again to be with his people. In the four verses of this ancient hymn and in the five we find in many church hymnals, we hear Jesus called by seven different names: Emmanuel; Wisdom from on high; Desire of nations; Lord of might; Rod of Jesse; Dayspring; and Key of David. Each of these titles reflects a different aspect of our Lord. As we continue our Advent journey, let us consider the many natures of Jesus, the one whose birth we are about to celebrate. Hear another prophecy given about the Messiah and the one who would prepare the hearts of the people to receive him. Zechariah spoke a prophecy about his own son, John the Baptist.

Reading: Luke 1:67-69, 76-79 (NRSV)

"Then his father Zechariah was filled with the Holy Spirit and spoke this prophecy: 'Blessed be the Lord God of Israel, for he has looked favorably on his people and redeemed them. He has raised up a mighty savior for us in the house of his servant David, as he spoke through the mouth of his holy prophets from of old ... And you, child, will be called the prophet of the Most High; for you will go

17

before the Lord to prepare his ways, to give knowledge of salvation to his people by the forgiveness of their sins. By the tender mercy of our God, the dawn from on high will break upon us, to give light to those who sit in darkness and in the shadow of death, to guide our feet into the way of peace.' "

Lighting Of The Advent Wreath And Reflection

Leader: And so, we light our first Advent candle in our wreath, the Prophecy Candle, remembering the voices who spoke of the birth of Messiah. We light our second Advent candle, the Bethlehem Candle, recognizing the fulfillment of Micah's prophecy of the place of our Lord's birth. Our third Advent candle, the Shepherds' Candle, acknowledges that God comes to the lowly, open hearts. Our fourth Advent candle, the Angels' Candle, which we will light next week recalls the angel who came to deliver to a virgin the news of a child to be born to her and the host of angels who proclaimed his birth. And Mary would travel with Joseph to a small town and there God's promises would be fulfilled. Let us sing "O Little Town Of Bethlehem" and hear of the love of God coming to earth in Jesus' birth.

Hearts Sing For Joy At The Birth Of Jesus

Congregational Song: "O Little Town Of Bethlehem" (vv. 1, 2)
O little town of Bethlehem,
How still we see thee lie!
Above thy deep and dreamless sleep
The silent stars go by;
Yet in thy dark streets shineth
The everlasting light;
The hopes and fears of all the years
Are met in thee tonight.

O holy Child of Bethlehem,
Descend to us we pray;

18

Cast out our sin, and enter in;
Be born in us today.
We hear the Christmas angels
The great glad tidings tell;
O come to us, abide with us,
Our Lord Emmanuel.
— Phillips Brooks (1835-1893)

Reflection

The author of this wondrous Christmas carol was an Episcopalian preacher who served congregations in Philadelphia and Massachusetts. This rather large man was an equally awesome preacher. Yet his heart was gentle and filled with love for children. In 1865 he journeyed to the Holy Land during the Christmas season. His spirit, so moved as he worshiped in the Bethlehem Church of the Nativity on Christmas Eve, inspired him three years later to compose this hymn for the children of his congregation to sing on Christmas Eve. How tender the words that tell the tale of the birthplace of our Lord, a town snuggled in the darkness of the night, a town to which a couple came and became parents of a Holy Child. Hear of the prophecy of Micah.

Reading: Micah 5:2, 4 (NRSV)

"But you, O Bethlehem of Ephrathah, who are one of the little clans of Judah, from you shall come forth for me one who is to rule in Israel, whose origin is from of old, from ancient days ... And he shall stand and feed his flock in the strength of the Lord, in the majesty of the name of the Lord his God."

Leader: And an angel appeared to the shepherds there on the plains of Bethlehem. He told them of the birth of Jesus. Then a host of angels burst into view singing praises to the newborn King. The shepherds ran to Bethlehem, racing through those dark streets, seeking the stable where Jesus was born. And they found the child, wrapped in swaddling cloths, and lying in a manger, a feeding trough for the animals. God's Son came to feed us, his people, with his own body and blood. Hear of his resting place that night.

19

Congregational Song: "Away In A Manger" (vv. 1, 2, 3)
Away in a manger, no crib for a bed,
The little Lord Jesus laid down his sweet head;
The stars in the sky looked down where he lay,
The little Lord Jesus, asleep on the hay.

The cattle are lowing, the Baby awakes,
But little Lord Jesus no crying he makes.
I love thee, Lord Jesus, look down from the sky,
And stay by my cradle till morning is nigh.

Be near me, Lord Jesus, I ask thee to stay
Close by me forever, and love me, I pray.
Bless all the dear children in thy tender care,
And fit us for heaven to live with thee there.
— Stanzas 1 and 2, Unknown
— Stanza 3, John Thomas McFarland (1851-1913)

Reflection

Today we have visions of a small babe in a different way. We see an infant, wrapped up in a warm blanket, lying on sheets of flannel, a mobile of animals hanging over the crib. The house is warm and cozy. Stuffed toys fill a basket nearby. A night light glows in the dark to calm the child if he should awaken. But the child this cradlesong speaks of did not have the comforts our children enjoy today. This song, by an unknown writer, is sung by children all over the world as a lullaby during the journey to Christmas. Mary wrapped her child up in bands of cloth and placed him in a cradle made for cattle to eat from, a manger. No sheets — a bed of straw to keep him warm. No stuffed sheep but live ones in a corner of the stable. But we become warm inside as we think of the little Lord Jesus, sleeping so peacefully. The song's last verse is a prayer asking our Lord to be near us in this life equipping us for our eternal resting place in heaven where Jesus and his Father will smile with love upon us, God's faithful children.

Reading: Galatians 4:4-6 (NRSV)
"But when the fullness of time had come, God sent his Son, born of a woman, born under the law, in order to redeem those who were under the law, so that we might receive adoption as children. And because you are children, God has sent the Spirit of his Son into our hearts, crying, 'Abba! Father!' "

Leader: We cry out to our Father, thanking him for the birth of his precious Son. Then we go, as the shepherds did, to adore him with our hearts. Let us declare that praise in the music of our next hymn, "Oh Come, All Ye Faithful."

Hearts Respond In Worship Of The Newborn King

Congregational Song: "Oh, Come, All Ye Faithful" (vv. 1, 2)
Oh, come, all ye faithful, joyful and triumphant,
Oh, come ye, oh, come ye to Bethlehem;
Come and behold him, born the king of angels;
Oh, come, let us adore him,
Oh, come, let us adore him,
Oh, come, let us adore him,
Christ the Lord!

Sing, choirs of angels, sing in exultation,
Oh, sing, all ye citizens of heaven above!
Glory to God, all glory in the highest;
Oh, come, let us adore him,
Oh, come, let us adore him,
Oh, come, let us adore him,
Christ the Lord!
— John F. Wade (1711-1786)

Reflection
This famous Christmas carol became popular after 1841 when the Reverend Frederick Oakeley made an English translation of the eighteenth century Latin hymn. The author of the original text is not known, but the music is attributed to an English organist, John

Reading. The hymn stirs the heart to come to that Bethlehem birth-place and worship Christ, our newborn King. Worship — the act of paying allegiance and giving honor to Jesus, our Lord. And how do we worship this great King? Hear God's Word.

Reading: John 4:23-24 (NRSV)
"But the hour is coming, and is now here, when the true worship-ers will worship the Father in spirit and truth, for the Father seeks such as these to worship him. God is spirit, and those who worship him must worship in spirit and truth."

Leader: We worship our Lord in the power of the Holy Spirit and in the truth that we are beloved children of God, made one with him through his precious Son, Jesus. So as our final act of worship, let us close with "Silent Night," a carol that has a wonderful story behind it. It appears that the Scripture that says, "In all things God works for good of those who love him, who have been called ac-cording to his purpose" (Romans 8:28), was fulfilled in a tiny Aus-trian town, in 1818. The organ had broken down, just before Christ-mas. But God had a plan and purpose to fulfill for the world in music. The parish priest and his organist worked frantically at com-posing lyrics and a tune that could be easily sung by their congre-gation with guitar instead of organ. Their hymn, "Silent Night," would probably not have been known outside of their village, if it weren't for the man sent to repair the organ. Hearing it played, he took a copy of the song and began sharing it with others. Soon touring groups picked it up, and eventually this work became one of the most beloved hymns we sing at Christmas. Yes, God has a way of working good to all who love him — in a song, in hearts open to receive their Lord, in a Child, born to us on a silent night so long ago. Let us rise and close with that blessed song.

Congregational Song: "Silent Night" (vv. 1, 2, 3)
    Silent night, holy night!
    All is calm, all is bright
    Round yon virgin mother and child.

22

Holy Infant, so tender and mild,
Sleep in heavenly peace,
Sleep in heavenly peace.

Silent night, holy night!
Shepherds quake at the sight;
Glories stream from heaven afar;
Heav'nly hosts sing, Alleluia!
Christ, the Savior, is born!
Christ, the Savior, is born!

Silent night, holy night!
Son of God, love's pure light
Radiant beams from thy holy face,
With the dawn of redeeming grace,
Jesus, Lord, at thy birth,
Jesus, Lord, at thy birth.
— Joseph Mohr (1792-1849)

Dismissal
Leader: Go in the love of the Son of God, born to us anew. Go in peace, and praise the Lord!
Congregation: Thanks be to God.

Postlude

Advent Bells

Foreword

Youth have a message to share about Jesus. This resource allows the youth of your congregation to ring their bells for their Savior. Advent is a time of fellowship. Invite families for a potluck meal or host a spaghetti supper. Have youth do the worship that night.

"Advent Bells" is an exciting worship geared to hearing about the preparation of Advent. The entire service may be done by the congregation's youth. A youth chorus sings special songs to proclaim the message of Advent. Christmas Jingle leads the group and interviews a variety of bell ringers. Congregational singing and readings from the Word involve all in this special Advent worship.

Advent Bells

A Midweek Advent Service For Youth

Welcome And Announcements

Prelude

Lighting Of The Advent Wreath

An Advent Call To Worship
Youth Leader

Congregational Song: "I Heard The Bells On Christmas Day"
(vv. 1-5)
>I heard the bells on Christmas day
>Their old familiar carols play,
>And wild and sweet the words repeat
>Of peace on earth, good will to men.
>
>I thought how, as the day had come,
>The belfries of all Christendom
>Had roll'd along th'unbroken song
>Of peace on earth, good will to men.
>
>And in despair I bow'd my head;
>"There is no peace on earth," I said,
>"For hate is strong, and mocks the song
>Of peace on earth, good will to men."
>
>Then pealed the bells more loud and deep;
>"God is not dead, nor doth he sleep;
>The wrong shall fail, the right prevail,
>With peace on earth, good will to men."

Till ringing, singing on its way,
The world revolved from night to day,
A voice, a chime, a chant sublime,
Of peace on earth, good will to men.
— Henry Wadsworth Longfellow (1807-1882)

Prayer Of The Day
Youth Leader: Let us pray. Stir up your Spirit in our world, O Lord, that it may be prepared to celebrate the birth of your Son once more. As the angels declared a Savior's birth, open our mouths to proclaim the birth of our King. Send us, like the shepherds, to others, excited to witness to your great love found in Jesus' coming to earth. Keep us wise, like the Magi, and strong in faith, like the apostles, until you come with the hosts of heaven to take us to our eternal reward. We pray in the name of the Child of Bethlehem, Jesus Christ our Lord.
Congregation: Amen. (*Congregation is seated*)

Congregational Song: "Ring Those Bells!" (Tune: "Jingle Bells")
Ring those bells, ring those bells!
Ring them loud and clear.
Let this Advent time proclaim a king is almost here.
Ring those bells, ring those bells,
Take time this Advent season
To proclaim our baby king, the reason for the season!

"Let's Ring Those Bells" Youth Skit

Leader

Congregational Song: "Prepare The Royal Highway" (vv. 1, 4)
Prepare the royal highway; the King of kings is near!
Let ev'ry hill and valley a level road appear!
Then greet the King of glory, foretold in sacred story:
Refrain: Hosanna to the Lord, for he fulfills God's Word!

27

His is no earthly kingdom; it comes from heav'n above.
His rule is peace and freedom and justice, truth, and love.
So let your praise be sounding for kindness so abounding:
Refrain: Hosanna to the Lord, for he fulfills God's Word!
— Franz M. Franzen (1772-1847)

Youth Chorus: "Oh, Advent Bells" (Tune: "Oh, Christmas Tree")

Chris Jingle

Alarm Clock Bells
Christmas Jingle (Chris) and Sleepy Head (Sleepy)

Reader 1: Isaiah 60:1 (NRSV)

Youth Chorus: "Oh, Advent Bells"

School Bells
Chris, Sleepy, and Teacher

Reader 2: 2 Timothy 4:1-3 (CEV)

Cow Bells
Chris and Cheerleaders

Youth Chorus: "Go, Tell It On The Mountain"

Congregational Song: "Little Jesus" (Tune: "Silver Bells")
Little Jesus, born of Mary
Came to us that first night.
In the air hosts of angels announced it.
Shepherds waiting, anticipating,
Heard the angels proclaim
That a Savior was born that day.

Chorus: Advent bells, Advent bells
It's Advent time in the church.
Ring-a-ling, hear them ring,
Soon we will see our king.

To the manger, did the shepherds
Fly with wings on their feet;
To a baby they knelt in adoration.
Having seen him with his mother,
They were captured by love,
And went forth to declare the Good News.
(Chorus)

Reading 3 (Narrator, Gabriel, and Mary): Luke 1:26-38 (CEV)

Youth Chorus: "Oh, Advent Bells"

Chris

Youth Chorus: "Oh, Advent Bells"

Jingle Bells And Door Bells
Chris; Jingle Bellers 1, 2, 3; and Door Bellers 1, 2, 3

Salvation Army Bells
Chris and Salvation Army Bell Ringer

Special Music

Offering

Handbells
Chris and Handbell Ringer

Alarm Bell

Chris

Reader 4: Luke 1:67-97 (CEV)

Congregational Song: "On Jordan's Banks The Baptist's Cry" (vv. 1, 2, 5)

> On Jordan's banks the Baptist's cry
> Announces that the Lord is nigh;
> Awake and hearken, for he brings
> Glad tidings of the King of kings!
>
> Then cleansed be ev'ry life from sin;
> Make straight the way for God within,
> And let us all our hearts prepare
> For Christ to come and enter there.
>
> All praise to you, eternal Son,
> Whose advent has our freedom won,
> Whom with the Father we adore,
> And Holy Spirit, evermore.
> — Charles Coffin (1676-1749)

Church Bells

Chris

Special Music by Junior or Congregational Bell Ringers

Dismissal Bells

Youth Chorus and All Players: "We Wish You A Blessed Advent" (Tune: "We Wish You A Merry Christmas")

Chris

Congregational Song: "Joy To The World" (vv. 1, 2, 3, 4)
Joy to the world, the Lord is come!
Let earth receive its King;
Let ev'ry heart prepare him room
And heav'n and nature sing,
And heav'n and nature sing,
And heav'n, and heav'n and nature sing.

Joy to the earth, the Savior reigns!
Let all their songs employ,
While fields and floods, rocks, hills, and plains
Repeat the sounding joy,
Repeat the sounding joy,
Repeat, repeat the sounding joy.

No more let sin and sorrow grow
Nor thorns infest the ground;
He comes to make his blessings flow
Far as the curse is found,
Far as the curse is found,
Far as, far as the curse is found.

He rules the world with truth and grace
And makes the nations prove
The glories of his righteousness
And wonders of his love,
And wonders of his love,
And wonders, wonders of his love.
— Isaac Watts (1674-1748)

Advent Dismissal And Benediction
Youth Leader: With joy in our hearts, let us go out into this Advent season and ring the Good News of Salvation with enthusiasm and conviction. Go, in the name of our Wonderful Counselor, our Powerful God, our Father Who Lives Forever, and the Prince of

Peace. In the name of the Father, Son, and Holy Spirit, go in peace and serve the Lord.
Congregation: Thanks be to God.

Postlude

Advent Bells

A Midweek Advent Service For Youth

Welcome And Announcements

Prelude

Lighting Of The Advent Wreath

An Advent Call To Worship
Youth Leader: Let us rise. Christmas day we celebrate the birth of
our Lord Jesus. Advent is the time to prepare for that day, a time to
ready our spirits to welcome God's Son into our world once more.
God's Holy Spirit calls us to prepare our hearts, to turn from our
sin, and to embrace God's salvation found in a baby. Hear the bells
call us to worship the Prince of Peace this Advent season. Come,
let us worship the Lord.

Congregational Song: "I Heard The Bells On Christmas Day"
(vv. 1-5)
    I heard the bells on Christmas day
    Their old familiar carols play,
    And wild and sweet the words repeat
    Of peace on earth, good will to men.

    I thought how, as the day had come,
    The belfries of all Christendom
    Had roll'd along th' unbroken song
    Of peace on earth, good will to men.

    And in despair I bow'd my head;
    "There is no peace on earth," I said,
    "For hate is strong, and mocks the song
    Of peace on earth, good will to men."

Then pealed the bells more loud and deep;
"God is not dead, nor doth he sleep;
The wrong shall fail, the right prevail,
With peace on earth, good will to men."

Till ringing, singing on its way,
The world revolved from night to day,
A voice, a chime, a chant sublime,
Of peace on earth, good will to men.
— Henry Wadsworth Longfellow (1807-1882)

Prayer Of The Day
Youth Leader: Let us pray. Stir up your Spirit in our world, O
Lord, that it may be prepared to celebrate the birth of your Son
once more. As the angels declared a Savior's birth, open our mouths
to proclaim the birth of our King. Send us, like the shepherds, to
others, excited to witness to your great love found in Jesus' coming to earth. Keep us wise, like the Magi, and strong in faith, like
the apostles, until you come with the hosts of heaven to take us to
our eternal reward. We pray in the name of the Child of Bethlehem,
Jesus Christ our Lord.
Congregation: Amen. (*Congregation is seated*)

Congregational Song: "Ring Those Bells!" (Tune: "Jingle Bells")
Ring those bells, ring those bells!
Ring them loud and clear.
Let this Advent time proclaim a king is almost here.
Ring those bells, ring those bells,
Take time this Advent season
To proclaim our baby king, the reason for the season!

"Let's Ring Those Bells" Youth Skit

Leader: It's time to ring those bells, so let's get set to ring in Advent by preparing ourselves and the road we'll travel.

Congregational Song: "Prepare The Royal Highway" (vv. 1, 4)
Prepare the royal highway; the King of kings is near!
Let ev'ry hill and valley a level road appear!
Then greet the King of glory, foretold in sacred story:
Refrain: Hosanna to the Lord, for he fulfills God's Word!

His is no earthly kingdom; it comes from heav'n above.
His rule is peace and freedom and justice, truth, and love.
So let your praise be sounding for kindness so abounding:
Refrain: Hosanna to the Lord, for he fulfills God's Word!
— Franz M. Franzen (1772-1847)

(Enter Youth, singing and ringing bells, dressed in hats and mufflers)

Youth Chorus: "Oh, Advent Bells" (Tune: "Oh, Christmas Tree")
Oh, Advent bells, oh, Advent bells,
We hear your music calling.
Oh, Advent bells, oh, Advent bells,
We hear your music calling.
You call us all to Bethlehem,
You call us all to be born again,
Oh, Advent bells, oh, Advent bells,
We know the Spirit's calling.

(Chorus groups at one side of sanctuary. All are carrying bells of some kind)

Chris Jingle: *(Steps out of the group, ringing jingle bells and singing)* "Jingle bells, jingle bells, jingle all the way ... oh, what fun we're going to have when we get to Christmas Day. Jingle bells, jingle bells, jingle all the way, but before we get there we need to stop along the way."
Hello there! Do you like my bells? I tie them to my door so I'll know who's entering my house. Their loud jingle announces I have a visitor. Tonight we will be hosts to a lot of visitors; especially

35

one unseen visitor, Jesus Christ our Lord. He needs no introduction for this is his house; but maybe I do.

I'm Christmas Jingle. Just call me Chris for short. My youth group is here to share a journey into the ding dong world of bells. As we travel down the path young people take during a day, let us remember that God is with us wherever we go, helping us ring the Good News of salvation to those who might not have heard it. Our first stop for a youngster is when he hears that alarm clock bell.

Alarm Clock Bells

Sleepy Head: (*Enters with an alarm ringing*) Oh, how I hate that alarm bell. I'm tired and don't want to get up. (*Shuts off alarm*)

Chris: Well, Sleepy, welcome to our Advent worship. We're glad you rose from your slumber. I was just reading in my morning devotions about rising and shining. Would you like to hear it too?

Sleepy: Okay, I need a pick-me-up from the Word. Let's hear it.

Reader 1: Isaiah 60:1 says, "Arise, shine for your light has come, and the glory of the Lord has risen upon you" (Isaiah 60:1 NRSV).

Sleepy: Rise? Shine? Well, my eyes still feel shut even with all this light. But look! What a group of people are gathered here! What did you say this was?

Chris: This is an Advent worship put on by your youth group. Its theme and focus are on bells. Do you realize we have just entered the season in the church year called Advent? And this group is here to help you begin your Advent journey.

Sleepy: I could use a jump start for my day. Maybe I should put on some music while I shower.

Chris: Well, your Advent choir has a song to sing which might help you wake up from your slumber. Hit it, chorus!

Youth Chorus: "Oh, Advent Bells" (Tune: "Oh, Christmas Tree")
Oh, Advent bells, oh, Advent bells,
We hear your music calling.
Oh, Advent bells, oh, Advent bells,
We hear your music calling.
    You call us all to Bethlehem,
    You call us all to be born again,
Oh, Advent bells, oh, Advent bells,
We know the Spirit's calling.

Sleepy: I'm sorry I'm so slow. My spirit's willing but this flesh is so weak. Why don't you come to school with me and maybe wake up a few people there with your enthusiasm and music?

Chris: Good idea. As Christians we are called to witness our faith in every area of our lives, not just at home. So, I'll see you in school. Don't be late!

School Bells

Teacher: (*Comes in ringing a school bell*) Come on, students. Don't be late. Rush, rush, rush, everyone is in a rush. Just calm yourself, now, (*says her name*). God has a lot out there for you today. These young people are a ripe field for God to plant seeds in. Today it's hard when you have to be careful about reaching out to others in love and sharing your faith with them. Teachers and students can't even pray publicly without getting into trouble. But I can pray for my classes in my own way. I can witness to my faith by doing a good job of preparation, being kind yet firm, and helping students when they need it. And listening ... just to listen to youth today helps them know someone cares.

But the crowd is coming so I better get prepared. Just a moment here (*bows head and prays silently*). Amen! There — I'm set for the day — Lord, I've committed it to you, so you're now in charge. (*Rings bell again*) Come on, kids, time to get started.

Chris: Advent is a time of preparation, a time to get set for Jesus' entry into our world once again. Preparation is a big part of that journey. Our high school teacher couldn't do a good job teaching if she wasn't prepared. She's prepared academically because she's read and researched her topic and has lesson plans prepared for her students. But this teacher is also prepared spiritually because she's committed her way to the Lord. God's Word gives Christians some careful instructions on this.

Reader 2: "When Christ Jesus comes as king, he will be the judge of everyone, whether they are living or dead. So with God and Christ as witnesses, I command you to preach God's message. Do it willingly, even if it isn't the popular thing to do. You must correct people and point out their sins. But also cheer them up, and when you instruct them, always be patient. The time is coming when people won't listen to good teaching. Instead, they will look for teachers who will please them by telling them only what they are itching to hear" (2 Timothy 4:1-3 CEV).

Chris: Being prepared — that's a big responsibility for Christians, not just teachers but students and all people — to be prepared to give an answer to those looking for Jesus. And that's what Advent is about — preparing ourselves by studying God's Word, by praying, and through worship. If we get set in those ways, we'll be excited about arriving at Christmas Day for it's time we've had in preparation which will help us ring in that day.

Cow Bells

Cheerleaders: (*come in waving pom poms and ringing cow bells*) Go, team, go! Go, team, go. We as Christians are called to go, go, go!

Chris: Well, it looks like we have some cheerleaders on God's team.

Lead Cheerleader: Yes, we're out there sharing the news of the birth of our Savior. Hit it, girls! Give me a J!

Squad: J!

Lead: Give me an E!

Squad: E!

Lead: Give me an S!

Squad: S!

Lead: Give me a U!

Squad: U!

Lead: Give me an S!

Squad: S!

Lead: And what does that spell?

Squad: Jesus!

Lead: And what's this season all about?

Squad: Jesus!

Chris: How right you are, God's Squad. During this season we are supposed to be out there proclaiming God's love coming to us in Jesus.

Lead: Yes, wherever we go, go, go (*rings bells*).

Cheerleader 1: We're to be out there telling others about the birth of Jesus and what it means to us today.

Cheerleader 2: And for me it means loving others as God loved me.

Cheerleader 3: And forgiving others just as God forgives me for goofing up.

Lead: Yes, God loves and forgives. Good news for young and old.

Chris: Well, that is pretty good news not just at Christmas time, but throughout the whole year. And where might we tell this Good News? Chorus, can you give us some direction?

Youth Chorus: "Go, Tell It On The Mountain"
    Go, tell it on the mountain, over the hills and ev'ry where;
    Go, tell it on the mountain, that Jesus Christ is born.

Chris: The night the shepherds heard the Good News they went to see for themselves and found Jesus, a baby. They encountered God's love and were transformed. Then they left to tell others.

Congregational Song: "Little Jesus" (Tune: "Silver Bells")
    Little Jesus, born of Mary
    Came to us that first night.
    In the air hosts of angels announced it.
    Shepherds waiting, anticipating,
    Heard the angels proclaim
    That a Savior was born that day.
    Chorus: Advent bells, Advent bells
    It's Advent time in the church.
    Ring-a-ling, hear them ring,
    Soon we will see our king.

    To the manger, did the shepherds
    Fly with wings on their feet;
    To a baby they knelt in adoration.
    Having seen him with his mother,
    They were captured by love,
    And went forth to declare the Good News.
    (Chorus)

Chris: Yes, there was excitement as the shepherds returned to their fields. I'm sure if they had cow bells back then they rang them. Advent is a time to prepare for Jesus' birth. Mary had been prepared by an angel the Bible tells us. Let us hear about her preparation.

Reading 3 (Narrator, Gabriel, and Mary read Luke 1:26-38 CEV):

Narrator: One month later God sent the angel Gabriel to the town of Nazareth in Galilee with a message for a virgin named Mary. She was engaged to Joseph from the family of King David. The angel greeted Mary and said ...

Gabriel: You are truly blessed! The Lord is with you.

Narrator: Mary was confused by the angel's words and wondered what they meant. Then the angel told Mary ...

Gabriel: Don't be afraid! God is pleased with you, and you will have a son. His name will be called Jesus. He will be great and will be the Son of God Most High. The Lord God will make him king, as his ancestor David was. He will rule the people of Israel forever, and his kingdom will never end.

Narrator: Mary asked the angel ...

Mary: How can this happen? I am not married!

Narrator: The angel answered ...

Gabriel: The Holy Spirit will come down to you, and God's power will come over you. So your child will be called the holy Son of God. Your relative Elizabeth is also going to have a son, even though she is old. No one thought she could ever have a baby, but in three months she will have a son. Nothing is impossible for God!

Narrator: Mary said ...

Mary: I am the Lord's servant! Let it happen as you have said.

Narrator: And the angel left her. (*Youth return to group*)

Chris: God prepared Mary, and God prepares us to receive Jesus, his Son. How does that tune go again, choir?

Youth Chorus: "Oh, Advent Bells" (Tune: "Oh, Christmas Tree")
Oh, Advent bells, oh, Advent bells,
We hear your music calling.
Oh, Advent bells, oh, Advent bells,
We hear your music calling.
You call us all to Bethlehem,
You call us all to be born again,
Oh, Advent bells, oh, Advent bells,
We know the Spirit's calling.

Chris: Yes, the Spirit calls us to be "born again" — to receive Christ anew. Just as Mary said, "Let it happen as you have said," God calls us to let him birth Jesus in our hearts. We carry the life of the Son of God in our hearts, and when the time comes for him to be delivered, it's awesome to see how we are transformed. Then our lives reflect that life. Just like these young bell ringers who are coming up as our chorus sings.

Youth Chorus: "Oh, Advent Bells" (Tune: "Oh, Christmas Tree")
Oh, Advent bells, oh, Advent bells,
We hear your music calling.
Oh, Advent bells, oh, Advent bells,
We hear your music calling.
You call us all to Bethlehem,
You call us all to be born again,
Oh, Advent bells, oh, Advent bells,
We know the Spirit's calling.

Jingle Bells And Door Bells

(Enter youth with jingle bells on sneakers and jump ropes and youth with door bells carrying grocery bags with food.)

Chris: And who might you be?

Jingle Beller 1: We're jumping for Jesus!

Jingle Beller 2: We've pledged to raise some money to help a mission project.

Jingle Beller 3: So we are *jingling* these bells to remind people that Christmas is a time to give not just get! *(Trio jumps up and down)*

Chris: *(Turns to the door bell ringers)* And what about you ringers? What kind of bells are those?

Door Beller 1: These are door bells. We're out gathering can goods and dry food stuff for the community food pantry.

Door Beller 2: It's a great opportunity to witness and wish people a Merry Christmas as we go house to house ringing our bells.

Door Beller 3: Lots of kids from school and area church groups do this to help people who don't have much receive Christmas baskets.

Salvation Army Bells

Chris: And here comes another bell ringer. I've seen a lot of these Salvation Army bell ringers out in the malls, in front of department stores, and in the entries of grocery stores.

Salvation Army Bell Ringer: Yes, we youth signed up to ring bells this Saturday from 8 a.m. to 8 p.m. We're going to ring in pairs and collect money for this organization so they can help those in need. Lots of people in our community and in our local church do this each year. I'm really excited about giving my time for this.

43

Chris: And I know the Salvation Army also collects foodstuff, toys, and outerwear as well. In fact, they have some people here tonight who are going to share a song to make our Advent journey a memorable one.

Special Music and Offering
(*Invite someone from your local Salvation Army branch to sing a song or give a special talk. If they are not musical, have some youth sing a special number during this time. Pass offering plates. Set up a kettle for members to drop in coins at the back of the church following the worship as well.*)

Chris: Thank you. The change we put in the Salvation Army pots helps others to have change in their lives by the work they do with those in need. Thank you all for becoming part of that work by your gifts. But, hold it, I see someone running in with another bell.

Handbells
Handbell Ringer: (*Enters ringing her bell*) Did I miss them? Did I miss them?

Chris: Who?

Handbell Ringer: The church bell ringers and choir. We're headed to the nursing homes to ring and sing. We want to bring God's love to shut-ins and others who can't get to church.

Chris: That's a great thing to do all year 'round, not just during Advent.

Handbell Ringer: You're right, but tonight we're off to visit and bring some Advent cheer to others. Ta-ta! I see the group loading up the bells to go. Wait for me! (*Rings bells as she leaves*)

Alarm Bell

Chris: I guess it's time for me to ring another bell. It's an alarm bell. We are called this Advent to listen to that baby born to Elizabeth, Mary's cousin. Her baby grew up to be known as John the Baptist, and as a prophet John sounded an alarm for people to wake up. When he was born, his father, Zechariah, spoke about the Savior to come and his son's role in preparing the way. Hear the Word of the Lord.

Reader 4: The Holy Spirit came upon Zechariah, and he began to speak: Praise the Lord, the God of Israel! He has come to save his people. Our God has given us a mighty Savior from the family of David his servant. Long ago the Lord promised by the words of his holy prophets to save us from our enemies and from everyone who hates us. God said he would be kind to our people and keep his sacred promise. He told our ancestor Abraham that he would rescue us from our enemies. Then we could serve him without fear by being holy and good as long as we live.

You, my son, will be called a prophet of God in heaven above. You will go ahead of the Lord to get everything ready for him. You will tell his people that they can be saved when their sins are forgiven. God's love and kindness will shine upon us like the sun that rises in the sky. On us who live in the dark shadow of death this light will shine to guide us into a life of peace (Luke 1:67-79 CEV).

Chris: And so we join those who over the centuries have heard the Baptist's cry announcing that Jesus is coming. Let us sing "On Jordan's Banks The Baptist's Cry."

Congregational Song: "On Jordan's Banks The Baptist's Cry" (vv. 1, 2, 5)
> On Jordan's banks the Baptist's cry
> Announces that the Lord is nigh;
> Awake and hearken, for he brings
> Glad tidings of the King of kings!

Then cleansed be ev'ry life from sin;
Make straight the way for God within,
And let us all our hearts prepare
For Christ to come and enter there.

All praise to you, eternal Son,
Whose advent has our freedom won,
Whom with the Father we adore,
And Holy Spirit, evermore.
— Charles Coffin (1676-1749)

Church Bells

Chris: And that brings us to our final bells: the church bells and our ringers have a song to share with you now as you recognize that this Advent you are free.

Special Music by Junior or Congregational Bell Ringers

Chris: Yes, on Christmas Day our church bells will announce that Jesus Christ is born, that peace has come to earth. However, as you hear those bells ring out remember that Jesus just doesn't come at Christmas, he's here all year 'round. So make this Advent a special bell ringing time, remembering to announce the Good News wherever you go.

Dismissal Bells

Youth Chorus and All Players: "We Wish You A Blessed Advent" (Tune: "We Wish You A Merry Christmas")
Chorus: We wish you a blessed Advent,
We wish you a blessed Advent,
We wish you a blessed Advent
And a joyous Christmas day.

Advent blessings to you,
And to all far and near.

Prepare yourselves
For the King is near.
(Chorus)

So come now, O Holy Spirit,
So come now, O Holy Spirit,
So come now, O Holy Spirit,
And show us the Lord.
(Chorus)

We can't wait until we see him,
We can't wait until we see him,
We can't wait until we see him,
And our praises we'll bring.
(Chorus)

Chris: And now from all of us in the youth group, your visitors in this night, and from Jesus, our unseen guest here, go forth and ring your bells with joy.

Congregational Song: "Joy To The World" (vv. 1, 2, 3, 4)
Joy to the world, the Lord is come!
Let earth receive its King;
Let ev'ry heart prepare him room
And heav'n and nature sing,
And heav'n and nature sing,
And heav'n, and heav'n and nature sing.

Joy to the world, the Savior reigns!
Let all their songs employ,
While fields and floods, rocks, hills, and plains
Repeat the sounding joy,
Repeat the sounding joy,
Repeat, repeat the sounding joy.

No more let sin and sorrow grow
Nor thorns infest the ground;

He comes to make his blessings flow
Far as the curse is found,
Far as the curse is found,
Far as, far as the curse is found.

He rules the world with truth and grace
And makes the nations prove
The glories of his righteousness
And wonders of his love,
And wonders of his love,
And wonders, wonders of his love.
— Isaac Watts (1674-1748)

(Youth Chorus and all participants except Youth Worship Leader go out during the singing of this carol. Line up in back to greet worshipers. Leader remains to give the dismissal and benediction.)

Advent Dismissal And Benediction
Youth Leader: With joy in our hearts, let us go out into this Advent season and ring the Good News of Salvation with enthusiasm and conviction. Go, in the name of our Wonderful Counselor, our Powerful God, our Father Who Lives Forever, and the Prince of Peace. In the name of the Father, Son, and Holy Spirit, go in peace and serve the Lord.
Congregation: Thanks be to God.

Postlude

We Welcome The Light Of Christmas

Foreword

This Christmas Eve worship resource is ideal for an early family worship experience. The resource consists of an order of worship, "We Welcome The Light Of Christmas," and skit, "The Christmas Light." Congregational singing prepares the worshipers to greet the Christ Child, sent from heaven to earth. A vocal solo frames the reading of the Word. Youth musicians (vocal, bells, or instrumental) are offered the opportunity to share their gifts between the reading of the lessons. The children are invited to come forward and gather around the pastor as they watch a skit. Four characters are involved: Angela the Christmas Angel, Dasher the Dog, Sorry the Sheep, and a Lost Shepherd. Costumes add color and make the skit realistic. An empty manger with straw and stuffed sheep around it can be a focal point. Dialogue centers on a lost frisbee which has turned into the Christmas star. Dasher the Dog retrieves Sorry the Sheep, and the Lost Shepherd comes looking for his sheep. Both hear the Good News in heaven and then return to earth to celebrate. Angela the Christmas Angel reveals her secret mission and helps the lost become found. She remains to help the pastor pass out gifts. Communion offers families the opportunity to celebrate this night of nights. The service ends with the singing of "Silent Night."

"We Welcome The Light Of Christmas" will be a memorable worship experience in the hearts of those seeking to grow closer to Jesus, the true Light of the World.

We Welcome The Light Of Christmas

Christmas Eve Service

Prelude

The Light Of God Appears

Call To Worship
Pastor: As the Wise Men saw the star in the east and came to worship the newborn king, let us rise and worship God's Son, Jesus the Christ, whose birth we celebrate this night.
Congregation: Come, let us welcome the light of Christmas.

Congregational Song: "The First Noel" (vv. 1, 2, 4)
    The first Noel, the angel did say,
    Was to certain poor shepherds in fields as they lay;
    In fields where they lay keeping their sheep,
    On a cold winter's night that was so deep.
    Noel, Noel, Noel, Noel!
    Born is the King of Israel.

    They looked up and saw a star
    Shining in the east, beyond them far;
    And to the earth it gave great light,
    And so it continued both day and night.
    Noel, Noel, Noel, Noel!
    Born is the King of Israel.

    This star drew near to the northwest,
    O'er Bethlehem it took its rest,
    And there it did both stop and stay,

Right over the place where Jesus lay.
Noel, Noel, Noel, Noel!
Born is the King of Israel.
— English Carol (seventeenth century)

Reading From The Gospel Of Matthew, The Second Chapter

Congregational Song: "O Little Town Of Bethlehem" (vv. 1, 2)
O little town of Bethlehem,
How still we see thee lie!
Above thy deep and dreamless sleep
The silent stars go by;
Yet in thy dark streets shineth
The everlasting light;
The hopes and fears of all the years
Are met in thee tonight.

For Christ is born of Mary,
And, gathered all above,
While mortals sleep, the angels keep
Their watch of wond'ring love.
O morning stars, together
Proclaim the holy birth,
And praises sing to God the king,
And peace to all the earth!
— Phillips Brooks (1835-1893)

The Prayer Of The Day
Pastor

Jesus, The Light Of God's Love

Solo: "Of The Father's Love Begotten" (v. 1)

Reading From The Gospel Of John, The First Chapter

Solo: "Of The Father's Love Begotten" (v. 3)

51

The Light Of God's Holy Word Shines On Our Hearts

First Lesson: Isaiah 9:2-7

Special Music (bells or youth choir/instrumentalist)

Second Lesson: Titus 2:11-14

Special Music

Congregational Song: "Angels, From The Realms Of Glory" (v. 1)
> Angels, from the realms of glory,
> Wing your flight o'er all the earth;
> Once you sang creation's story;
> Now proclaim Messiah's birth:
> *Come and worship, come and worship,*
> *Worship Christ, the newborn king.*
> — James Montgomery (1771-1854)

The Gospel Announced
Pastor: The Gospel according to Saint Luke, the second chapter.
Congregation: Glory to you, O Lord.

The Gospel Proclaimed: Luke 2:1-20
Pastor: The Gospel of the Lord.
Congregation: Praise to you, O Christ.

Congregational Song: "Angels, From The Realms Of Glory" (v. 2)
> Shepherds, in the fields abiding,
> Watching o'er your flocks by night,
> God with us is now residing,
> Yonder shines the infant light.
> *Come and worship, come and worship,*
> *Worship Christ, the newborn king.*

Children Invited Forward

The Light Of Heaven Comes Down To Earth

Congregational Song: "Angels We Have Heard On High" (vv. 1, 2, 3)
> Angels we have heard on high,
> Sweetly singing o'er the plains,
> And the mountains in reply
> Echoing their joyous strains.
> *Gloria in excelsis Deo;*
> *Gloria in excelsis Deo.*
>
> Shepherds, why this jubilee?
> Why your joyous strains prolong?
> What the gladsome tidings be
> Which inspire your heav'nly song?
> *Gloria in excelsis Deo;*
> *' Gloria in excelsis Deo.*
>
> Come to Bethlehem and see
> Him whose birth the angels sing;
> Come, adore on bended knee
> Christ the Lord, the newborn king.
> *Gloria in excelsis Deo;*
> *Gloria in excelsis Deo.*
> — French Carol

Children's Skit: *The Christmas Light*
Angela the Christmas Angel, Dasher the Dog, Sorry the Sheep, the Lost Shepherd

Children Return To Pews

The Angels Announce The Birth Of Pure Light

Congregational Song: "Hark! The Herald Angels Sing" (vv. 1, 3)
> Hark! The herald angels sing,
> "Glory to the newborn king;

Peace on earth, and mercy mild,
God and sinners reconciled."
Joyful, all you nations, rise;
Join the triumph of the skies;
With angelic hosts proclaim,
"Christ is born in Bethlehem!"
Hark! The herald angels sing,
"Glory to the newborn king!"

Hail the heav'n born Prince of Peace!
Hail the Sun of Righteousness!
Light and life to all he brings,
Ris'n with healing in his wings.
Mild he lays his glory by,
Born that we no more may die,
Born to raise each child of earth,
Born to give us second birth.
Hark! The herald angels sing,
"Glory to the newborn king!"
— Charles Wesley (1707-1788)

Pastor's Reflection On Children's Skit

We Respond To The Light

Confession of Faith: The Apostles' Creed*
I believe in God, the Father almighty,
    creator of heaven and earth.
I believe in Jesus Christ, his only Son, our Lord.
        He was conceived by the power of the Holy Spirit
            and born of the Virgin Mary.
        He suffered under Pontius Pilate,
            was crucified, died, and was buried.
        He descended to the dead.
        On the third day he rose again.

*If available, you may want to use The Christmas Creed here.

He ascended into heaven,
   and is seated at the right hand of the Father.
He will come again to judge the living and the dead.
I believe in the Holy Spirit,
   the holy catholic Church,
   the communion of saints,
   the forgiveness of sins,
   the resurrection of the body,
   and the life everlasting. Amen.

Prayers Of The Church

Pastor: Let us pray for the whole people of God, in Christ Jesus, and for all people according to their needs. For the light which is shed upon our hearts as we welcome the birth of Jesus in our world once again. Lord in your mercy,
Congregation: Touch us with the light of Christmas.
Pastor: For the renewing of faith and the empowering of our congregation to witness to the transforming light of Christ in our midst. Lord in your mercy,
Congregation: Touch us with the light of Jesus, your Son.
Pastor: For the strengthening of family relationships and the healing of broken hearts and words that have wounded. Lord in your mercy,
Congregation: Touch us with the desire and power to forgive.
Pastor: For those in our midst who need your help and healing touch, especially we pray for those we raise before you and those on our prayer list ... (*petitions may be offered*). Lord in your mercy,
Congregation: Touch them with the power of your love.
Pastor: Lord, we praise you for hearing our prayers and shining your light into our midst and into all situations. In the name of the Christ Child of Bethlehem, we pray.   .
Congregation: Amen.

Offering

Offering Music: "It Came Upon The Midnight Clear," "Good Christian Friends, Rejoice," "Go, Tell It On The Mountain"

Offertory

We Feed On God's Light

Eucharistic Prayer

Words Of Institution

The Lord's Prayer

The Distribution Of Communion

Communion Music: "Oh, Come, All Ye Faithful," "Away In A Manger," "What Child Is This?" "We Three Kings Of Orient Are"

Communion Prayer
Pastor: Now may the body and blood of our Lord Jesus Christ strengthen you and keep you in his grace.
Congregation: Amen.
Pastor: Let us pray. Jesus, you left the glory of heaven and came to earth to reside in the hearts of your people. Your mother placed you in a manger, a feeding trough for animals. Thank you for touching our hearts with your love and for feeding us tonight with your body and blood. You gave your life as a sacrifice for us, enable us to live in grateful response to your gift. In your holy name we pray.
Congregation: Amen.

The Light Shines In The Darkness

(During the singing of "Silent Night," the lights are dimmed. If desired, a group of older youth may light candles in front of the congregation as they begin singing.)

56

Congregational Song: "Silent Night" (vv. 1, 2, 3)
Silent night, holy night!
All is calm, all is bright
Round yon virgin mother and child.
Holy Infant, so tender and mild,
Sleep in heavenly peace,
Sleep in heavenly peace.

Silent night, holy night!
Shepherds quake at the sight;
Glories stream from heaven afar;
Heav'nly hosts sing, Alleluia!
Christ, the Savior, is born!
Christ, the Savior, is born.

Silent night, holy night!
Son of God, love's pure light
Radiant beams from thy holy face,
With the dawn of redeeming grace,
Jesus, Lord, at thy birth,
Jesus, Lord, at thy birth.
— Joseph Mohr (1792-1849)

Benediction
Pastor: The light of our Lord's love has come to us in the birth of God's Son, who brings us salvation. May the blessing of that Good News go with us now as we celebrate Jesus, the Light of the World.
Congregation: Let the light shine!
Pastor: Go into this world as lights shining with joy. Go in the name of the Father, the Son, and the Holy Ghost.
Congregation: We go with joy in our hearts! Amen.
(Lights are brightened and/or candles extinguished.)

The Light Goes Out To The World

Congregational Song: "Joy To The World" (vv. 1, 2, 3, 4)
Joy to the world, the Lord is come!
Let earth receive its King;
Let ev'ry heart prepare him room
And heav'n and nature sing,
And heav'n and nature sing,
And heav'n, and heav'n and nature sing.

Joy to the earth, the Savior reigns!
Let all their songs employ,
While fields and floods, rocks, hills, and plains
Repeat the sounding joy,
Repeat the sounding joy,
Repeat, repeat the sounding joy.

No more let sin and sorrow grow
Nor thorns infest the ground;
He comes to make his blessings flow
Far as the curse is found,
Far as the curse is found,
Far as, far as the curse is found.

He rules the world with truth and grace
And makes the nations prove
The glories of his righteousness
And wonders of his love,
And wonders of his love,
And wonders, wonders of his love.
— Isaac Watts (1674-1748)

Pastor: Go in the peace of the Child of Bethlehem. Go in his love
and serve the Lord.
Congregation: Glory to God in the Highest!

Postlude

We Welcome The Light Of Christmas

Christmas Eve Service

Prelude

The Light Of God Appears

Call To Worship
Pastor: As the Wise Men saw the star in the east and came to worship the newborn king, let us rise and worship God's Son, Jesus the Christ, whose birth we celebrate this night.
Congregation: Come, let us welcome the light of Christmas.

Congregational Song: "The First Noel" (vv. 1, 2, 4)
The first Noel, the angel did say,
Was to certain poor shepherds in fields as they lay;
In fields where they lay keeping their sheep,
On a cold winter's night that was so deep.
Noel, Noel, Noel, Noel!
Born is the King of Israel.

They looked up and saw a star
Shining in the east, beyond them far;
And to the earth it gave great light,
And so it continued both day and night.
Noel, Noel, Noel, Noel!
Born is the King of Israel.

This star drew near to the northwest,
O'er Bethlehem it took its rest,
And there it did both stop and stay,
Right over the place where Jesus lay.

59

Noel, Noel, Noel, Noel!
Born is the King of Israel.
— English Carol (seventeenth century)

Reading From The Gospel Of Matthew, The Second Chapter
"Jesus was born in the town of Bethlehem in Judea during the time when Herod was king. When Jesus was born, some wise men from the east came to Jerusalem. They asked, 'Where is the baby who was born to be the king of the Jews? We saw his star in the east and have come to worship him.' When King Herod heard this, he was troubled, as well as all the people in Jerusalem. Herod called a meeting of all the leading priests and teachers of the law and asked them where the Christ would be born. They answered, 'In the town of Bethlehem in Judea. The prophet wrote about this in the Scriptures: "But you, Bethlehem, in the land of Judea, are important among the tribes of Judah. A ruler will come from you who will be like a shepherd for my people Israel" ' " (Matthew 2:1-6 NCV).

Congregational Song: "O Little Town Of Bethlehem" (vv. 1, 2)
O little town of Bethlehem,
How still we see thee lie!
Above thy deep and dreamless sleep
The silent stars go by;
Yet in thy dark streets shineth
The everlasting light;
The hopes and fears of all the years
Are met in thee tonight.

For Christ is born of Mary,
And, gathered all above,
While mortals sleep, the angels keep
Their watch of wond'ring love.
O morning stars, together
Proclaim the holy birth,
And praises sing to God the king,
And peace to all the earth!
— Phillips Brooks (1835-1893)

60

The Prayer Of The Day

Pastor: Father in heaven, we welcome the light of Christmas, Jesus your Son. Jesus, you are the pure light of God's love. Shine your light into our hearts that we would turn from the darkness of our sin and embrace the light of your grace. Jesus, you were born to rescue us from sin and death. To you be all honor and glory, now and forever. Amen.

Jesus, The Light Of God's Love

Solo: "Of The Father's Love Begotten" (v. 1)
    Of the Father's love begotten,
    Ere the worlds began to be,
    He is Alpha and Omega,
    He the source, the ending he,
    Of the things that are, that have been,
    And that future years shall see,
    Evermore and evermore.
    — Prudentius (348-413)

Reading From The Gospel Of John, The First Chapter

"In the beginning there was the Word. The Word was with God, and the Word was God. He was with God in the beginning. All things were made by him, and nothing was made without him. In him there was life, and that life was the light of all people. The Light shines in the darkness, and the darkness has not overpowered it ... The Word became a human and lived among us. We saw his glory — the glory that belongs to the only Son of the Father — and he was full of grace and truth" (John 1:1-5, 14 NCV).

Solo: "Of The Father's Love Begotten" (v. 3)
    This is he whom seers in old time
    Chanted of with one accord,
    Whom the voices of the prophets
    Promised in their faithful word;

Now he shines, the long expected;
Let creation praise its Lord
Evermore and evermore.

The Light Of God's Holy Word Shines On Our Hearts

First Lesson: Isaiah 9:2-7

Special Music (bells or youth choir/instrumentalist)

Second Lesson: Titus 2:11-14

Special Music

Congregational Song: "Angels, From The Realms Of Glory" (v. 1)
> Angels, from the realms of glory,
> Wing your flight o'er all the earth;
> Once you sang creation's story;
> Now proclaim Messiah's birth:
> *Come and worship, come and worship,*
> *Worship Christ, the newborn king.*
> — Jamrs Montgomery (1771-1854)

The Gospel Announced
Pastor: The Gospel according to Saint Luke, the second chapter.
Congregation: Glory to you, O Lord.

The Gospel Proclaimed: Luke 2:1-20
Pastor: The Gospel of the Lord.
Congregation: Praise to you, O Christ.

Congregational Song: "Angels, From The Realms Of Glory" (v. 2)
> Shepherds, in the fields abiding,
> Watching o'er your flocks by night,

God with us is now residing,
Yonder shines the infant light.
Come and worship, come and worship,
Worship Christ, the newborn king.

Children Invited Forward

The Light Of Heaven Comes Down To Earth

Congregational Song: "Angels We Have Heard On High" (vv. 1, 2, 3)

Angels we have heard on high,
Sweetly singing o'er the plains,
And the mountains in reply
Echoing their joyous strains.
Gloria in excelsis Deo;
Gloria in excelsis Deo.

Shepherds, why this jubilee?
Why your joyous strains prolong?
What the gladsome tidings be
Which inspire your heav'nly song?
Gloria in excelsis Deo;
Gloria in excelsis Deo.

Come to Bethlehem and see
Him whose birth the angels sing;
Come, adore on bended knee
Christ the Lord, the newborn king.
Gloria in excelsis Deo;
Gloria in excelsis Deo.
— French Carol

Children's Skit: *The Christmas Light*
Angela the Christmas Angel, Dasher the Dog, Sorry the Sheep, the
Lost Shepherd (*See page 69.*)

Children Return To Pews

The Angels Announce The Birth Of Pure Light

Congregational Song: "Hark! The Herald Angels Sing" (vv. 1, 3)
    Hark! The herald angels sing,
    "Glory to the newborn king;
    Peace on earth, and mercy mild,
    God and sinners reconciled."
    Joyful, all you nations, rise;
    Join the triumph of the skies;
    With angelic hosts proclaim,
    "Christ is born in Bethlehem!"
    Hark! The herald angels sing,
    "Glory to the newborn king!"

    Hail the heav'n born Prince of Peace!
    Hail the Sun of Righteousness!
    Light and life to all he brings,
    Ris'n with healing in his wings.
    Mild he lays his glory by,
    Born that we no more may die,
    Born to raise each child of earth,
    Born to give us second birth.
    Hark! The herald angels sing,
    "Glory to the newborn king!"
    — Charles Wesley (1707-1788)

Pastor's Reflection On Children's Skit

We Respond To The Light

Confession of Faith: The Apostles' Creed*
I believe in God, the Father almighty,
    creator of heaven and earth.
I believe in Jesus Christ, his only Son, our Lord.
    He was conceived by the power of the Holy Spirit
        and born of the Virgin Mary.
    He suffered under Pontius Pilate,
        was crucified, died, and was buried.
    He descended to the dead.
    On the third day he rose again.
    He ascended into heaven,
        and is seated at the right hand of the Father.
    He will come again to judge the living and the dead.
I believe in the Holy Spirit,
    the holy catholic Church,
    the communion of saints,
    the forgiveness of sins,
    the resurrection of the body,
    and the life everlasting. Amen.

Prayers Of The Church

Pastor: Let us pray for the whole people of God, in Christ Jesus, and for all people according to their needs. For the light which is shed upon our hearts as we welcome the birth of Jesus in our world once again. Lord in your mercy,
Congregation: Touch us with the light of Christmas.
Pastor: For the renewing of faith and the empowering of our congregation to witness to the transforming light of Christ in our midst. Lord in your mercy,
Congregation: Touch us with the light of Jesus, your Son.
Pastor: For the strengthening of family relationships and the healing of broken hearts and words that have wounded. Lord in your mercy,

*If available, you may want to use The Christmas Creed here.

65

Congregation: Touch us with the desire and power to forgive.
Pastor: For those in our midst who need your help and healing touch, especially we pray for those we raise before you and those on our prayer list ... (*petitions may be offered*). Lord in your mercy,
Congregation: Touch them with the power of your love.
Pastor: Lord, we praise you for hearing our prayers and shining your light into our midst and into all situations. In the name of the Christ Child of Bethlehem, we pray.
Congregation: Amen.

Offering

Offering Music: "It Came Upon The Midnight Clear," "Good Christian Friends, Rejoice," "Go, Tell It On The Mountain"

Offertory

We Feed On God's Light

Eucharistic Prayer

Words Of Institution

The Lord's Prayer

The Distribution Of Communion

Communion Music: "Oh, Come, All Ye Faithful," "Away In A Manger," "What Child Is This?" "We Three Kings Of Orient Are"

Communion Prayer
Pastor: Now may the body and blood of our Lord Jesus Christ strengthen you and keep you in his grace.
Congregation: Amen.
Pastor: Let us pray. Jesus, you left the glory of heaven and came to earth to reside in the hearts of your people. Your mother placed

you in a manger, a feeding trough for animals. Thank you for touching our hearts with your love and for feeding us tonight with your body and blood. You gave your life as a sacrifice for us, enable us to live in grateful response to your gift. In your holy name we pray. **Congregation: Amen.**

The Light Shines In The Darkness

(During the singing of "Silent Night," the lights are dimmed. If desired, a group of older youth may light candles in front of the congregation as they begin singing.)

Congregational Song: "Silent Night" (vv. 1, 2, 3)
Silent night, holy night!
All is calm, all is bright
Round yon virgin mother and child.
Holy Infant, so tender and mild,
Sleep in heavenly peace,
Sleep in heavenly peace.

Silent night, holy night!
Shepherds quake at the sight;
Glories stream from heaven afar;
Heav'nly hosts sing, Alleluia!
Christ, the Savior, is born!
Christ, the Savior, is born.

Silent night, holy night!
Son of God, love's pure light
Radiant beams from thy holy face,
With the dawn of redeeming grace,
Jesus, Lord, at thy birth,
Jesus, Lord, at thy birth.
— Joseph Mohr (1792-1849)

Benediction
Pastor: The light of our Lord's love has come to us in the birth of God's Son, who brings us salvation. May the blessing of that Good News go with us now as we celebrate Jesus, the Light of the World.
Congregation: Let the light shine!
Pastor: Go into this world as lights shining with joy. Go in the name of the Father, the Son, and the Holy Ghost.
Congregation: We go with joy in our hearts! Amen.
(Lights are brightened and/or candles extinguished.)

The Light Goes Out To The World

Congregational Song: "Joy To The World" (vv. 1, 2, 3, 4)
Joy to the world, the Lord is come!
Let earth receive its King;
Let ev'ry heart prepare him room
And heav'n and nature sing,
And heav'n and nature sing,
And heav'n, and heav'n and nature sing.

Joy to the earth, the Savior reigns!
Let all their songs employ,
While fields and floods, rocks, hills, and plains
Repeat the sounding joy,
Repeat the sounding joy,
Repeat, repeat the sounding joy.

No more let sin and sorrow grow
Nor thorns infest the ground;
He comes to make his blessings flow
Far as the curse is found,
Far as the curse is found,
Far as, far as the curse is found.

He rules the world with truth and grace
And makes the nations prove
The glories of his righteousness
And wonders of his love,
And wonders of his love,
And wonders, wonders of his love.
— Isaac Watts (1674-1748)

Pastor: Go in the peace of the Child of Bethlehem. Go in his love and serve the Lord.
Congregation: Glory to God in the Highest!

Postlude

Skit

The Christmas Light

Participants:
Angela the Christmas Angel
Dasher the Dog
Sorry the Sheep
The Lost Shepherd
Pastor

(*Dress skit participants appropriately. Dasher and Sorry come running down the aisle. Sorry wears a bell that jingles around her neck and hangs onto a leash that Dasher holds as he runs.*)

Angela: (*Enters the pulpit singing*) "Angels we have heard on high, sweetly singing o'er the plains ..." I'm in great voice tonight, and look, I even have an audience all assembled to hear me sing. Hello, young people. I'm Angela the Christmas Angel, and I'm looking for a lost frisbee. I was practicing with my dog, Dasher, for the Heavenly Playoffs, and I tossed it out into space, but it didn't come back. Have you seen it?

Dasher: (*Comes running down the aisle with a sheep in tow*) I found it! I found it! Woof! Woof! I found it!

Angela: Oh, Dasher, this is great. But this wooly thing doesn't look like our frisbee. Kids, what do you think this is? (*Children respond, "A sheep!"*)

Sorry: Baa! Baa! You're right, children. I'm not a frisbee. I'm Sorry.

Angela: Oh, what are you sorry for?

Sorry: Baa! Baa! No, I'm not sorry for anything. My name is Sorry. Sorry the Sheep. Who are you? Where am I?

Angela: Oh, your name is Sorry. Well, my name is Angela the Christmas Angel, and this — why, this is heaven!

Sorry: Heaven! Have I died?

Angela: I don't think so. I sent my dog Dasher to find our lost frisbee, and he's come back to me with a little lost sheep.

Sorry: Baa! Baa! Yes, I'm lost. Baa! Baa!

Angela: Why are you crying, little sheep?

Sorry: Baa! Baa! I'm lost and can't find my shepherd!

Shepherd: (*Steps out carrying a staff*) Here I am, Sorry. I had quite a time getting here, but I've finally arrived. Where are we?

Angela: You're in heaven.

Shepherd: Heaven! Have I died?

Angela: I don't think so. I sent my dog Dasher to find our lost frisbee, and he's come back to me with a little lost sheep and now a shepherd.

Shepherd: A *lost* sheep and a *lost* shepherd, I might add.

Angela: Two *lost* souls. Well, this is the right spot for you both. Heaven is for those who were lost and then found. But I'm getting ahead of my story. Let me introduce myself. I'm Angela the Christmas Angel, and I was just about to leave heaven and go to earth. I had this frisbee, see. I tossed it out into the heavens, and it disappeared. But wait! Could that be it way out there? See that bright shining light out there, kids? (*Light appears in a dark area of the church — balcony, back of the church, or so forth. Star prop may be used with flashlight.*) That brilliant new star just popped into space over that tiny little town of Bethlehem.

Shepherd: Why is that light so special?

Angela: Well, that light is headline news — God's announcement to the world about what he has just done for it. You see, the Lord has sent me on a mission tonight.

Shepherd: God is sending an angel on a mission to our lost world? Could that really be possible?

Angela: I realize that your world is quite a mess, but this mission to save it is not impossible. God really loves the world and has a wonderful plan to save it. And it all begins tonight. But I have to hurry. I have an appointment with a bunch of shepherds on the hills surrounding that town you see the star over — the little town of Bethlehem. I'm going to tell them some very good news.

Sorry: Baa! I'm sorry; I don't understand. What good news are you going to bring to us down there on earth?

Angela: See that manger? (*Points to an empty manger*) Well, tonight that Bethlehem manger will be filled with a child.

Sorry: I'm soooo sorry. A baby in a manger. That's a place for all the animals to eat out of — not a very nice place to put a newborn child.

Angela: I know that. But because there's no room in any of the inns in Bethlehem tonight, Mary and Joseph had to go to a stable. Mary's the young woman who has just brought that baby boy into the world. She's put him in a manger to keep him safe and warm.

Sorry: Baa! I'm sorry. What a place for a little baby to be put.

Angela: But this is no ordinary baby. This is a king.

Sorry: A *newborn* king. Wow! Baa! I'm impressed!

Angela: Well, he's not just a king. This little baby is God's Son.

Sorry: God's Son. Oh, well then, *I'm really sorry* that he has to come into the world like that.

Angela: Well, you don't have to be sorry, little lost one. God is reaching out to all the lost tonight. That baby came into the world to save all people. That little child will be called Jesus, and he will become the Savior of the world.

Shepherd: Well, that is good news! Come on, Sorry, let's get home quickly so that we can tell others.

Angela: Don't say a word yet. Just return to earth and wait for me to come. You've just had a preview of what is about to happen. The star in the east that just appeared will be seen by many. And some will wonder at its light. But the real light will be found in that baby lying in the manger. Jesus is the real light, the light which shines in the darkness, the true light from God. But I'm off now, kids, so I'll let the pastor continue my tale. Remember, you heard it first right here in church. That's where you find a lot of good news. Come on, Dasher. Bring Sorry and our shepherd. I'll wing you home. Merry Christmas!

Pastor: Wow! Stay a minute, Christmas Angel. I could use your help. (*Dasher, Sorry, and Shepherd go off. Angela stays to help pass out gifts.*)

Wasn't that great, children? It was like going to the movies and looking back almost 2,000 years, remembering that first night when Jesus was born. Our Christmas Angel was the one who came and told those lowly shepherds that Jesus Christ was born. And do you know what they did when they heard that Good News? They ran as fast as they could to Bethlehem, and there they saw the baby Jesus just as the angel told them. That star shone so bright that night because God wanted to get the world's attention. He had great news to declare to all people. And this Christmas night we tell it also. Jesus came as the Light of the world, a babe born to rescue those who say they are sorry for doing bad things, to save those who are lost. And when Jesus grew up, he became the Good Shepherd. The Lord is our shepherd, and he is still with us, guiding us, forgiving us when we do wrong, and calling us to remember how much God loves us. So let's go out this Christmas and be God's lights, shining out to others in love.

(*Pass out gifts — angels, ornaments, candy canes, WWJD bracelets in red and green.*)